COMPUTER SECURITY GUIDE

Protecting Your Digital Life

Ray Goodwin

CONTENTS

LIABILITY DISCLAIMER

The information contained within this book is intended for informational purposes only and should not be construed as legal or professional advice. The authors and publishers of this book are not responsible for any losses or damages that may arise from the use of the information contained within.

The reader assumes full responsibility for any decisions made based on the information in this book. The authors and publishers do not endorse any particular method, service or product mentioned in this book and are not responsible for any consequences resulting from their use.

The reader should exercise caution and discretion when making life changing decisions, and should be aware of the risks and potential consequences of their actions. This book is not a substitute for professional or legal advice and should not be relied upon as such.

By reading and using the information in this book, the reader acknowledges and agrees to hold harmless the authors, publishers, and any other parties involved in the creation or distribution of this book from any and all liability, claims, damages, or losses that may arise from their use of the information contained herein.

CHAPTER 1: INTRODUCTION TO COMPUTER SECURITY

Welcome to the Computer Security Guide! In today's digital age, it has become increasingly important to protect our personal information from cyber threats. With more and more people conducting their everyday activities online, we are all vulnerable to cyber-attacks that could compromise our finances, identity, and reputation.

As someone who has worked in the tech industry for over two decades, I have seen firsthand how crucial it is to have a solid understanding of computer security. In this book, I will guide you through the best practices for protecting yourself and your devices from online threats.

We will cover everything from securing your passwords and personal accounts to protecting your home network from potential hackers. You will also learn about malware, phishing scams, and other common tactics used by cybercriminals.

But don't worry - you don't need to be a tech expert to understand this guide. I have kept it simple so that anyone can follow along and implement these security measures into their daily routine.

By following the tips in this guide, you can rest assured that you are taking proactive steps towards keeping yourself safe online. Let's get started!

Overview

In today's world, technology has become inseparable from our lives. From smartphones to laptops, we are constantly connected to the internet, which has transformed the way we work, communicate, and do business.

However, with every advancement comes a new set of challenges. One critical issue that is ever-present is the need for computer security. We entrust our personal and professional assets to the digital world, and we need to ensure that they are adequately protected. This is the purpose of computer security.

What is Computer Security?

Computer security is the practice of protecting digital assets against unauthorized access, theft, damage and disruption. It is a broad field that encompasses cybersecurity, data protection, network security, application security, mobile device security, cloud security, and many others.

In simpler terms, computer security involves safeguarding information and systems from malicious attacks, hackers, and other security threats.

Importance of Computer Security

The importance of computer security cannot be overstated. In today's world, we heavily rely on technology for nearly every aspect of our lives. Our data, private information, and intellectual property are all vulnerable to attack, and the cost of such incidents could be significant.

The damage to reputation, loss of revenue, and fines can have a severe impact on businesses and individuals alike. Additionally, there could be legal and ethical implications to consider when dealing with data breaches and loss of sensitive information.

Therefore, it is crucial to invest in computer security measures to mitigate the risk of such incidents and protect critical data and assets.

Types of Computer Security Threats

There are many types of computer security threats that can cause damage and disruption to digital systems and assets. Some of the common threats include:

❖ Malware attacks: This includes viruses, worms, Trojan horses, ransomware, spyware, and adware. These attacks can infect systems and devices, causing data breaches, identity theft, and financial losses.

❖ Phishing attacks and social engineering: This involves the use of fraudulent emails, websites, and messages that disguise as legitimate sources to trick individuals into divulging private information. These attacks can lead to identity theft and financial loss.

❖ Denial-of-service (DoS) attacks: In this type of attack, the hacker overwhelms a system with traffic, causing the system to become slow or unresponsive.

❖ Insider threats: This refers to malicious or unintentional harm caused by individuals within an organization. It could include data theft, equipment sabotage, or sharing confidential information outside of the organization.

❖ Physical security threats: This includes theft, natural disasters, fires, and other environmental disruptions.

❖ Cyberterrorism and cyber warfare: These attacks are politically motivated, targeting governments and large-scale organizations, intending to cause chaos and damage.

❖ Advanced persistent threats (APTs): APTs are long-term targeted attacks that could infiltrate systems unnoticed and remain undetected for long periods.

❖ Cloud-based security threats: This is a relatively new challenge that organizations face. It involves the security risks associated with storing data on remote servers outside of an organization's network.

Common Misconceptions about Computer Security

There are many misconceptions about computer security that could lead individuals and organizations to adopt the wrong security strategies. Some of the most common myths include:

➤ We are too small to be a target: This is a false assumption that many small businesses make. However, hackers often target small organizations to gain access to larger ones within their network.

➤ Antivirus software is enough: While having antivirus software is essential, it is not enough to provide comprehensive security to a network.

➤ Cybersecurity is only for IT professionals: Cybersecurity is not just for IT personnel. All individuals within an organization have a role in maintaining data security.

➤ A strong password is enough: While having a strong password is an integral part of data security, there are other critical factors such as two-factor authentication, use of encryption, and regular patching of systems that need to be considered.

Basic Principles of Computer Security

There are some fundamental principles of computer security that should be considered when addressing cybersecurity risks. These include:

❖ Confidentiality: Confidentiality involves protecting

information from unauthorized access, disclosure, or theft. This principle ensures that sensitive data is only accessible to authorized persons.

❖ Integrity: The integrity principle ensures that data is accurate, consistent and trustworthy, and has not been subject to modification or tampering.

❖ Availability: Availability ensures that data and resources are available to authorized users when needed.

❖ Non-repudiation: This principle ensures that an individual cannot deny taking a specific action, such as sending an email or approving a financial transaction.

❖ Authentication: This principle involves verifying the identity of users accessing a network or system, typically through the use of usernames and passwords.

Benefits of Good Computer Security Practices

Good computer security practices benefit individuals and organizations in many ways, including:

➤ Protecting data integrity: Good computer security practices ensure that data is accurate and consistent, maintaining the trustworthiness of the information.

➤ Mitigating the risk of financial loss: Data breaches and cyber-attacks can cause significant financial losses. Good computer security practices can help to reduce the likelihood and impact of such incidents.

➤ Protecting reputation: Data breaches and cyber-attacks can severely damage an organization's reputation. Strong computer security practices can reduce the likelihood of such incidents and ensure that an organization's reputation remains intact.

➢   Maintaining business continuity: In case of a cyber incident, it is critical to maintain business continuity and recover swiftly. Good computer security practices help to lessen the impact and ensure that an organization can continue operating despite the incident.

Key Stakeholders in Computer Security

The responsibility of computer security goes beyond the IT department. All employees, senior management, and stakeholders have a role to play in ensuring that proper security measures are implemented.

IT personnel are responsible for implementing security measures and ensuring that systems are secure and up to date. Senior management is responsible for making security a priority and investing resources in cybersecurity. Employees are responsible for adhering to security protocols and alerting IT personnel when they detect anything suspicious.

Historical Evolution of Computer Security

The history of computer security can be traced back to the 1960s when the primary concern was securing time-sharing systems from unauthorized access. As computer systems evolved, security threats also became more sophisticated. Factors such as the development of the internet and the increasing reliance on technology for everyday activities have led to new security challenges.

The evolution of computer security has been driven by the need to address emerging threats. Today, computer security is an essential aspect of our digital lives. As technology continues to evolve, so will the challenges and opportunities in computer security. It is essential to remain vigilant and adapt to changing threats to ensure that we are adequately protected.

CHAPTER 2: THREATS TO COMPUTER SECURITY

Computer security threats come in all shapes and sizes. They can be as simple as a phishing email that tricks users into giving away their passwords or as complex as a nation-state-sponsored cyberattack that aims to disrupt critical infrastructure. In this chapter, we will discuss some of the most common types of computer security threats and their impact on organizations and individuals.

Malware attacks are among the most prevalent and damaging computer security threats. Malware is a broad term that includes computer viruses, worms, Trojans, ransomware, spyware, and adware. These malicious programs are designed to damage or disrupt computer systems, steal information, or extort money from victims.

Viruses are self-replicating programs that attach themselves to legitimate files and spread through email attachments, infected software, or other means. They can cause damage to system files, slow down computer performance, and spread to other machines on the network.

Worms are similar to viruses, but they do not require a host file to spread. They can infect computers by exploiting vulnerabilities in software or operating systems. Once they infect a computer, they can spread quickly to other machines on the network, causing widespread damage and disruption.

Trojans are programs that disguise themselves as legitimate software but contain hidden malicious code. They can be used to steal sensitive information, spy on users, or give hackers access to infected machines.

Ransomware is a type of malware that encrypts files on a victim's computer and demands payment in exchange for the decryption key. This type of attack has become increasingly common in recent years and can have a devastating impact on organizations that rely on sensitive data.

Spyware and adware are programs that are designed to track users' online activities and display unwanted ads or pop-ups. They can also steal personal information, such as credit card numbers and passwords.

Phishing attacks and social engineering are another common type of computer security threat. Phishing emails or websites are designed to trick users into sharing sensitive information, such as usernames, passwords, or credit card numbers. Social engineering attacks use psychological manipulation to trick users into divulging sensitive information or performing a malicious action.

Denial-of-service (DoS) attacks are designed to make a website or network unavailable by flooding it with traffic or other forms of disruption. These attacks can cause significant damage to organizations that rely on their online presence to conduct business.

Insider threats are security risks that come from within an organization. These can be intentional or unintentional, and they can be caused by employees, contractors, or other trusted individuals who have access to sensitive data or systems.

Physical security threats include theft, natural disasters, and fire. These threats can cause significant damage to computer systems and can lead to data loss, downtime, or other negative consequences.

Cyberterrorism and cyberwarfare are emerging threats that are becoming increasingly sophisticated and widespread. Nation-state-sponsored attacks can target critical infrastructure, such as power grids, transportation systems, or financial networks, and can cause widespread disruption and damage.

Advanced persistent threats (APTs) are targeted attacks that are designed to evade detection and gain access to sensitive information or systems. This type of attack can be difficult to detect and can remain hidden for long periods of time.

Cloud-based security threats are another emerging threat that can have significant consequences for organizations that rely on cloud services for data storage or computing power. These threats can include unauthorized access, data breaches, and attacks on cloud infrastructure or services.

In conclusion, computer security threats are numerous and diverse. Organizations and individuals need to be aware of these threats and take appropriate measures to protect their systems and data. This includes implementing security best practices, keeping software and systems up-to-date, and staying informed about emerging threats and vulnerabilities. In the next chapter, we will discuss vulnerabilities and exploits and how they can be used by attackers to compromise computer systems and networks.

CHAPTER 3: VULNERABILITIES AND EXPLOITS

Computer systems have become a part of our daily lives. By providing services that span across financial, educational, social, medical, and many other domains, these systems have made life convenient and comfortable. However, these systems are also vulnerable to attacks from different kinds of malicious actors. Therefore, it has become imperative for computer users to understand the vulnerabilities and exploits that plague these systems. This chapter discusses in detail the various vulnerabilities that systems are susceptible to and how these vulnerabilities are exploited to gain unauthorized access.

Vulnerabilities are weaknesses in the design, implementation, or configuration of a system that can be exploited by an attacker. These vulnerabilities can be introduced at various levels, such as the application, operating system, firmware, or hardware. They could also be software-based or hardware-based in nature. Unfortunately, vulnerabilities are not always intentional and can sometimes be the result of incomplete testing or lack of resources. The challenge for businesses and individuals is to identify and address these vulnerabilities before an attacker exploits them.

One common way of identifying vulnerabilities is through vulnerability scanning. Vulnerability scanning involves the automated testing of software or hardware to identify known vulnerabilities. These tests could be performed on the operating system, applications, or network infrastructure. Vulnerability scanning can be either passive or active. In passive scanning, the scanner only listens to the network traffic, while in active scanning, the scanner actively sends packets to the destination in question.

Once a vulnerability is identified, an attacker will try to exploit it by sending specially crafted data to the system. Exploits are specific techniques or tools used by attackers to take advantage of vulnerabilities in a system or application. Attackers use exploits to gain unauthorized access to a system or to cause the system to behave in an unexpected manner. The use of exploits is a popular technique among attackers because it allows them to gain access to a system without using complex or sophisticated attacks.

One of the most popular exploit techniques is buffer overflow. A buffer overflow attack occurs when a program writes more data to a buffer than it can accommodate. In such cases, the excess data will overflow into adjacent memory areas, sometimes overwriting important data. This situation could lead to the system crashing or the attacker executing arbitrary code on the system, leading to remote code execution.

Another popular technique used by attackers is SQL (Structured Query Language) injection. This exploit involves inserting SQL commands into a query to access, modify, or delete data from a database. SQL injection attacks can result in data theft, data manipulation, and loss of confidentiality, integrity, and availability of data.

Cross-site scripting (XSS) is another common exploit technique used by attackers. This technique involves injecting malicious code into websites viewed by unsuspecting users. When users visit these websites, the malicious code is executed on their browsers, giving attackers unauthorized access to sensitive information such as passwords, cookies, and other sensitive data.

Zero-day exploits represent a significant security challenge because they exploit vulnerabilities for which no patches or remediation strategies exist. A zero-day attack is so named because the targeted software vendor has had zero days to patch or release a fix for the vulnerability. These exploits are particularly effective because they are virtually unknown to the vendor, antivirus software, and security communities.

Organizations can use threat modelling to identify potential vulnerabilities in their systems. Threat modelling is a structured process of identifying, analysing, and prioritizing potential threats and vulnerabilities to a system. In threat modelling, stakeholders can identify and prioritize the assets that need protection, the likely attackers, the potential vulnerabilities, and the impacts of various attack scenarios. With the information gathered, organizations can prioritize the vulnerabilities that pose the most significant risks and budget resources accordingly.

Patch management is another important aspect of vulnerability mitigation. Patch management involves keeping software up-to-date with the latest patches and upgrades. Vendors frequently release patches to address known security vulnerabilities and flaws. It is essential to apply these patches as soon as possible and to stay current with the latest software releases. Timely patching can help to reduce the impact of security breaches.

Balancing security and usability is a challenge for system designers. Security measures, such as firewalls and antivirus software, can sometimes be too restrictive and reduce the usability of the system. For example, requiring users to change their passwords every week could reduce the usability of the system. Therefore, a balance must be struck between security and usability. For example, organizations can use adaptive security, where security measures are adjusted based on the context in which they are used.

In conclusion, understanding vulnerabilities and exploits is crucial to the task of securing computing systems. Identifying vulnerabilities, using threat modelling, and timely patching are essential steps in mitigating vulnerabilities. Additionally, it is critical to balance security and usability to ensure that systems remain usable while remaining secure. By taking these steps, organizations and individuals can significantly reduce the risk of security breaches by malicious actors.

CHAPTER 4: AUTHENTICATION AND ACCESS CONTROL

Authentication and access control are vital mechanisms used in cybersecurity that ensure that only authorized personnel can access certain networks, programs, applications, and data, among other systems. Effective authentication and access control techniques are essential since unauthorized access, misuse of data, or the compromise of system integrity may lead to dire consequences such as financial loss, reputational damage, or loss of life. In this chapter, we will explore the principles and best practices of authentication and access control, including password-based authentication, two-factor authentication, multi-factor authentication, biometric authentication, role-based access control, access control models, access control lists, and capabilities-based security.

Principles of Authentication and Access Control

Authentication serves as the first line of defence against unauthorized access to information systems. Authentication involves verifying that a user is who they claim to be, commonly by requiring a username and a password. The password is a secret shared between the user and the system, and it should never be shared with any other person or written down where someone else can discover it. Other types of authentication include two-factor authentication, biometric authentication, and using a smart card or other physical token.

Access control includes various mechanisms that limit who, when, where, and under what conditions a user can access information or perform particular actions within an information system. Access control mechanisms can be:

❖ Role-based access control (RBAC): This assigns access permissions based on job roles, hence preventing permission escalation or bureaucratic hurdles.

❖ Access control models: Discretionary, mandatory, and role-based access control are examples of access control models.

Password-Based Authentication - Best Practices and Pitfalls

Passwords are the most commonly used authentication method and are critical components of security. However, passwords can be vulnerable to attacks since most people do not use strong passwords or maintain them securely. Some of the best practices for secure password usage include:

❖ Length - using lengthy passwords, which are a minimum of 12 characters, contains letters, numbers, and symbols, ensures that passwords are difficult to guess.

❖ Avoiding reuse - using the same password across multiple accounts could lead to the user's exposure in the occurrence of a data breach.

❖ Avoiding predictable words - using predictable words such as names, locations, or birthdays make it easier for hackers to guess passwords.

❖ Using two-factor or multi-factor authentication for increased password security.

Two-Factor Authentication (2FA) and Multi-Factor

Authentication (MFA)

Two-factor authentication is a security process in which users must provide two different authentication factors before they are granted access. An example is when a user is required to provide a password and a unique code sent via SMS, email, or a mobile app. Two-factor authentication ensures that the system knows that the person is authorized to access data since two different types of authentication factors are used.

Multifactor authentication involves the use of more than two types of authentication factors, which include biometric authentication and smart cards. Multifactor authentication ensures added security since a user needs to have a password, a physical token, and a password sent through an SMS.

Biometric Authentication - Pros and Cons

Biometric authentication involves using physiological or behavioural features to verify a user's identity. These features include fingerprints, face recognition, and retinas patterns. Biometric authentication provides an added layer of security since it is difficult to forge, but it can be expensive to deploy.

Single Sign-On (SSO) and Federated Identity Management

Single sign-on involves the use of a single authentication procedure to gain access to multiple systems. This method significantly reduces the number of passwords and usernames users must remember. Federated identity management combines single sign-on systems with other enterprise applications to create an easy-to-manage centralized system to help manage user's access and authentication across various systems.

Role-Based Access Control (RBAC)

Role-based access control (RBAC) is an access control system that assigns permissions to users based on their job functions. RBAC ensures that users only have access to the minimum amount of information necessary to perform their role. Suppose a user moves to another role. In that case, their access rights can be easily updated, ensuring continued security.

Access Control Models - Discretionary, Mandatory, and Role-Based Access Control

Access control models address the issue of who has permission to access certain resources in a system. The three common access control models include:

❖ Discretionary access control (DAC) - permission to access a resource is granted by the resource owner. DAC is mostly used in small organizations, and it is prone to manipulation since any user can grant others access, they may not require.

❖ Mandatory access control (MAC) - access rights are assigned by the system or security administrator. MAC ensures that users do not have excessively high-level permissions. However, it may restrict access to some user's duties and responsibilities.

❖ Role-based access control (RBAC) - this assigns access permissions based on job roles, hence preventing permission escalation or bureaucratic hurdles.

Access Control Lists (ACLs) and Capabilities-Based Security

Access control lists (ACLs) and capabilities-based security are methods of granting access control to users. An access control list sets permissions for various resources for each user or group of users. While capabilities-based security permits access to resources based on the user's cryptographic capability or the specific key.

In conclusion, authentication, and access control are essential mechanisms that secure information systems. These mechanisms range from simple password authentication to multi-factor authentication, including biometric and smart card authentication. Access control requires the implementation of policies such as DAC, MAC, or RBAC and control mechanisms such as ACLs and capabilities-based security. The discussion in this chapter emphasizes the need to deploy these mechanisms in the fight against cyber threats to secure information systems.

CHAPTER 5: NETWORK SECURITY

The internet has revolutionized the way businesses operate today, and its role in the global economy is ever-increasing. With computers interconnected worldwide, it has become paramount to ensure the security of computer networks. Network security is critical for protecting vital organizational data from malicious attacks. This chapter is all about network security—the hardware, software, and procedures that ensure the confidentiality, availability, and integrity of transmitted data across network devices like routers, switches, and firewalls.

Network architecture and layout

Network architecture refers to the physical and logical structure of a network. Network layout is the positioning of the network infrastructure, like switches, routers, and access points, the network topology, including the way in which the devices are linked, and their connection to the internet.

Physical network security demands are driven by a company's particular geographic situation and vulnerabilities. Organizations with offices in dangerous neighbourhoods or areas wide open to the public will need a heightened level of security to ensure that unauthorized individuals do not get physical access to the networking hardware.

Logical network security, in contrast, concentrates more on the configuration of the software. Logical structures include user IDs, authentication protocols, authorization, and access controls. These logical structures inside your network add extra layers of safety and manage access to the physical network of the business.

Network protocols and standards

Network protocols are the rules and techniques used to connect networking devices and transmit data between them. Some of them include Transmission Control Protocol/Internet Protocol (TCP/IP), File Transfer Protocol (FTP), Simple Mail Transfer Protocol (SMTP), and Hypertext Transfer Protocol (HTTP). Proper protocol management helps to eliminate vulnerabilities and enhancing the security of the network.

Devices used in network security

Various devices can be employed to protect a network's perimeter from external threats. Here are the most common network security devices:

Firewalls: These are the most common networking device for securing a network's perimeter. They set up a barrier between the organization's internal network and other untrusted networks such as the internet and different WAN connections. Firewalls evaluate incoming and outgoing traffic, and only authorized traffic is allowed to pass through.

Switches: Switches connect and divide internal networks within an organization. These devices forward data packages just to the targeted devices. Typically, they only support connections for wired devices, such as servers and desktop computers, as well as wired peripherals.

Routers: Routers allow communication between multiple networks by forwarding packets of data sent between different networks. Using rules and protocols, routers route network traffic to the appropriate endpoint.

Intrusion Detection and Prevention Systems (IDS/IPS): This hardware or software monitors network traffic to determine if it contains malicious activity. If an attack is detected, these systems can provide actionable intelligence for security incident response measures.

Perimeter security

Perimeter security is a crucial aspect of network security. It establishes layers of defence around the network to minimize unauthorized access to it. It involves deploying security measures that protect private network resources from third-party access. Some related security measures are:

Firewalls: A firewall serves as the gateway that screens and controls incoming and outgoing traffic between two networks. It prevents unauthorized users and cybercriminals from accessing the network while ensuring that authorized users can access the resources they require.

VPN: A virtual private network (VPN) is a private connection between an endpoint, such as a device, and a VPN server over the internet. It encrypts data and hides it from untrusted internet service providers and bad actors that may try to intercept it.

Intrusion Detection and Prevention Systems (IDS/IPS): IDS/IPS systems are instrumental in inspecting network traffic to identify malicious packets or data. This is because cybercriminals often use packet manipulation to launch their attacks, and it may not be visible to standard security programs.

Wireless network security

Wireless networks pose unique security risks because they are accessible to anyone within range. Wi-Fi traffic can be intercepted by attackers, so it must be encrypted to prevent unauthorized access. Some effective security measures for wireless networks include:

WEP: Wired Equivalent Privacy (WEP) is a security protocol designed for wireless networks that encrypts data before sending it over the airwaves. However, it is no longer considered secure.

WPA: Wi-Fi Protected Access (WPA) is a Wi-Fi security protocol that helps keep wireless data private. It uses Advanced Encryption Standard (AES) for data encryption, making it significantly more secure than WEP.

WPA2: Wi-Fi Protected Access 2 (WPA2) is currently the most popular security protocol for Wi-Fi networks. It uses a stronger encryption algorithm than WPA.

Network isolation and segmentation

Network isolation and segmentation are practices that involve dividing a network into smaller sections to minimize an attacker's "blast radius." This limits the damage in case an attacker gains access to a particular network segment. It also adds extra layers of security to the network as a whole by isolating the elements from each other. Different technologies are used to implement network segmentation, including:

VLANs: Virtual Local Area Networks (VLANs) are isolated broadcast domains in a switched network. A VLAN separates a network into several different logical networks that are isolated from each other, allowing you to limit access to particular network resources.

Subnets: Subnetting is dividing a network into smaller, more manageable subnetworks. It is mostly used to divide a massive network into smaller ones to make it more manageable.

Virtual Private Networks (VPNs): VPNs permit remote users to connect to a private network across the internet by encrypting the traffic and hiding it from any unauthorized viewing.

Network monitoring and incident response

Network monitoring is the act of regularly inspecting network traffic to identify abnormal activity that may indicate an intrusion or breach. With the use of proper security information controls and Network Access Controls, network administrators can view the types of traffic being exchanged, and who is using the network to create a comprehensive overview of the network. This oversight periodical network assessment helps security teams distinguish abnormal behaviours, identify common attack routes like web access, and ultimately limit data breaches. Incident response is the process utilized to manage an attack on the network when it is occurring. It begins with preparing and completing a business continuity plan (BCP), assessing the situation, and stopping the ongoing threats. The network admin then moves to contain the impact along with reporting to clients and management before performing evidence collection, resolution, and monitoring.

Conclusion

Network security is paramount to an organization's safety and security. With the increased risks of cyber-attacks, network security devices' proper selection and deployment stand as the barrier to keep organizations safe. The proper implementation of the discussed security firewalls, routers, switches, and intrusion prevention ads an additional layer of security to your networks. Additionally, analysis and periodical test help to identify gaps and reduce risks in your networks.

CHAPTER 6: APPLICATION SECURITY

In today's world, almost every company uses web applications in some capacity. From banking to healthcare, education to entertainment, and everything in between, web applications serve as the backbone of many businesses. Unfortunately, web applications are also one of the most common targets for cyber attackers. Therefore, it is essential to understand the principles of application security.

The Open Web Application Security Project (OWASP) is a community-driven organization that provides resources and tools for web application security. They have developed a list of the top 10 web application security risks that every organization should be aware of. This list is a great starting point for understanding the most common vulnerabilities in web applications.

The first risk on the OWASP list is Injection. Injection attacks occur when attackers inject malicious code into a web application, typically through user input fields. This type of attack allows the attacker to execute malicious code on vulnerable web servers, which can lead to data leaks, data destruction, or even a complete system takeover. Injection attacks can be prevented by using input validation techniques and using prepared statements when communicating with a database.

The second risk on the OWASP list is Broken Authentication and Session Management. This risk occurs when web applications do not properly authenticate users, or they do not handle user session data correctly. Attackers can exploit these vulnerabilities to access sensitive data or take over user sessions. Good authentication practices include the use of strong passwords, multi-factor authentication, and the use of secure session management techniques.

The third risk on the OWASP list is Cross-Site Scripting (XSS). XSS is a type of injection attack that targets the client-side code of a web application, allowing attackers to run malicious code on a user's machine. This type of attack can be prevented by validating user input and sanitizing user-generated content before sending it to the client.

The fourth risk on the OWASP list is Insecure Direct Object References. This type of vulnerability occurs when developers expose object references (for example, user IDs or file names) directly, without validating the user's authorization to access them. Attackers can exploit these vulnerabilities to gain unauthorized access to sensitive data, modify data, or execute arbitrary code. Developers can prevent these vulnerabilities by implementing access controls that validate user authorization for every object reference.

The fifth risk on the OWASP list is Security Misconfiguration. This vulnerability occurs when developers do not properly configure web applications, such as web servers, databases, or frameworks. Attackers can exploit these vulnerabilities to gain unauthorized access to sensitive data or take control of the system. Developers can prevent these vulnerabilities by making sure that every component of a web application is properly configured before it is deployed.

The sixth risk on the OWASP list is Sensitive Data Exposure. This vulnerability occurs when developers do not properly protect sensitive data, such as passwords, credit card numbers, or personal information. Attackers can exploit these vulnerabilities to gain access to sensitive data, which can lead to identity theft, financial fraud, and other types of cybercrime. Developers can prevent these vulnerabilities by using secure encryption protocols and taking steps to prevent sensitive data from being stored or transmitted in cleartext.

The seventh risk on the OWASP list is Broken Access Controls. This type of vulnerability occurs when web applications do not properly implement access controls. Attackers can exploit these vulnerabilities to gain unauthorized access to sensitive data, modify data or execute malicious code. Implementing access control mechanisms like role-based access control (RBAC) can help mitigate these risks.

The eighth risk on the OWASP list is Insufficient Attack Protection. This risk occurs when web applications do not have adequate protection against common attack methods, like brute force attacks, cross-site request forgery (CSRF), or clickjacking. Implementing security measures such as rate limiting, CSRF tokens, and avoiding deprecated security mechanisms like Flash or ActiveX can all help reduce these risks.

The ninth risk on the OWASP list is Insecure Cryptographic Storage. This type of vulnerability occurs when web applications store sensitive data in an insecure manner. Attackers can exploit these vulnerabilities to gain access to sensitive data like passwords, financial data, and other confidential records. Developers can prevent these vulnerabilities by using strong encryption protocols and hashing algorithms to secure sensitive data.

The tenth risk on the OWASP list is Insecure Communications. This risk occurs when web applications do not secure communication between clients and servers or between servers. Attackers can exploit these vulnerabilities to intercept sensitive data, such as login credentials or financial data. Developers can prevent these vulnerabilities by using secure communication protocols like SSL/TLS and using modern encryption algorithms.

In addition to following OWASP's recommendations, developers should also implement secure software development practices that prioritize security from the start. This includes techniques such as threat modelling, secure coding practices, code reviews, and continuous testing and assessment of security vulnerabilities.

It is also important to take third-party libraries and frameworks into consideration. Developers must assess and mitigate the risks of using open-source libraries, ensuring that they are updated regularly and come from trusted sources.

In conclusion, application security is a vital aspect of computer security, with web applications being a frequent target for cyber attackers. The OWASP Top Ten list is an excellent starting point for understanding the most common vulnerabilities in web applications and the best practices for mitigating those risks. Developers must develop secure software development practices, follow proper authentication and session management techniques, and take steps to prevent vulnerabilities from occurring to keep their web applications safe and secure. As technologies evolve and threats become more complex, it is essential to stay up-to-date on best practices and techniques to protect your web applications and keep your clients' sensitive data safe.

CHAPTER 7: DATA SECURITY AND PRIVACY

Data security and privacy are of paramount importance to individuals, businesses, and governments. Over the years, there have been numerous cases of data breaches and loss of personal and sensitive information, leading to financial loss, identity theft, and reputational damage. As such, it is necessary to understand the importance of data security and privacy, the types of sensitive data, data classification, data retention policies, data backup, disaster recovery planning, data encryption and decryption, database security, and privacy laws and regulations.

Importance of Data Security and Privacy

Data security and privacy are essential in protecting sensitive information from unauthorized access, modification, theft, and loss. By ensuring data security and privacy, individuals and businesses can mitigate the risks associated with data breaches, unauthorized data access, and theft. Additionally, data security and privacy build trust between organizations and their customers, employees, and partners.

Types of Sensitive Data

Sensitive data includes personal information, financial

information, health information, and confidential business information, among others. Personal information includes names, addresses, email addresses, social security numbers, and date of birth. Financial information includes credit card numbers, bank account details, and investment portfolios. Health information includes medical records, insurance information, and prescription details. Confidential business information includes trade secrets, intellectual property, and financial statements.

Data Classification and Labelling

Data classification is the process of assigning a level of sensitivity or importance to data based on its criticality, confidentiality, or value. The classification system can be critical, sensitive, or public, depending on the level of importance or sensitivity of the data. Critical data is confidential and must be protected from unauthorized access, whereas public data is freely available. Data labelling allows users to know the level of sensitivity of the data and how to handle it.

Data Retention Policies and Procedures

Data retention policies define how long data is kept and the process of disposing of it. The policies ensure that data is not kept for longer than necessary, and it reduces the risk of data loss or theft. Data retention policies must comply with the privacy laws, regulations, and industry standards.

Data Backup and Disaster Recovery Planning

Data backup is essential in ensuring that data can be recovered in case of loss, theft, or damage. Data backup must be done regularly and stored in a secure location in case of a disaster. Disaster recovery planning ensures that the organization can recover from a disaster and continue with normal operations.

Data Encryption and Decryption

Data encryption is the process of converting data into a format that cannot be read or understood without a decryption key. Encryption ensures that data is secure, even if it is intercepted by an unauthorized person. Data decryption is the process of converting encrypted data back into its original form.

Database Security

Database security is the protection of data stored in databases from unauthorized access, modification, theft, or loss. Access control, data encryption, and auditing are essential in ensuring database security.

Privacy Laws and Regulations

Privacy laws and regulations are designed to protect sensitive data and ensure that individuals and organizations comply with the rules. The laws include the General Data Protection Regulation (GDPR), the California Consumer Privacy Act (CCPA), the Health Insurance Portability and Accountability Act (HIPAA), and the Children's Online Privacy Protection Act (COPPA), among others.

Conclusion

Data security and privacy are critical components of computer security. Users must understand the importance of data security and privacy, the types of sensitive data, data classification, data retention policies, data backup, disaster recovery planning, data encryption and decryption, database security, and privacy laws and regulations. By ensuring data security and privacy, individuals, businesses, and governments can protect sensitive information from unauthorized access, modification, theft, and loss.

CHAPTER 8: MOBILE DEVICE SECURITY

With the rapid proliferation of smartphones and tablets, mobile devices represent a significant security threat for individuals and businesses alike. Hackers and cybercriminals are constantly devising new ways to exploit vulnerabilities in mobile devices, including the operating system, apps, and network connections. In this chapter, we will explore various mobile security threats and risks, and discuss the best practices for securing your mobile devices.

Mobile Security Threats and Risks

Mobile devices face numerous security threats, including malware infections, stolen data, and network intrusions. Here are some of the most common mobile security threats and risks to be aware of:

1. Malware: Mobile malware is on the rise, with hackers developing viruses, worms, and Trojans that specifically target mobile devices. Malware can access and steal sensitive information, such as passwords, location data, and personal contacts, and can also cause your device to crash or become unusable.

2. Data theft: In the event that your mobile device is lost or stolen, there's a risk that sensitive data stored on it could be compromised. Cybercriminals can access your data by simply stealing your device, or even by intercepting data as it is transmitted wirelessly. This makes it important to encrypt sensitive data and choose strong passwords for your mobile device.

3. Network intrusions: Using public Wi-Fi networks, which are often unsecured, can expose you to serious security threats. Mobile devices that connect to an unsecured public Wi-Fi network can be vulnerable to network intrusions, where hackers can intercept and read your data traffic. To protect your mobile device from such network intrusions, you should use a VPN app that encrypts all network traffic.

4. Phishing: Phishing scams are commonly used to trick mobile users into giving up personal information, such as login credentials or credit card details. Phishing scams can be delivered via text message or email, and often appear to be from a legitimate source, like a bank or online retailer.

Mobile Device Management and Mobile Application Management

Mobile device management (MDM) and mobile application management (MAM) are two closely related technologies that can help protect mobile devices. MDM involves managing mobile devices such as smartphones and tablets, usually within a business or enterprise setting, to secure and control access to sensitive data. MAM, on the other hand, involves managing mobile apps, typically for individuals or small businesses, to ensure that sensitive data remains secure.

Mobile Operating System Security

The operating system (OS) is crucial when it comes to mobile security since it is the foundation that the device is built upon. iOS and Android are the most popular mobile operating systems, with both having their own security features and vulnerabilities.

iOS is considered to be one of the most secure mobile operating systems due to its closed software structure and stringent app review process, which prevent apps from accessing sensitive data without user permission. It also offers a range of security features such as device encryption, two-factor authentication, and remote wipe.

Android, on the other hand, is an open-source platform, which means that individual manufacturers can customize the software to their specific hardware requirements. This can lead to security vulnerabilities since not all Android devices receive timely security updates, which could expose them to newly discovered vulnerabilities. Additionally, Android has proven to be more susceptible to malware attacks than iOS.

Mobile Device Encryption

Encrypting your device is an important security measure since it scrambles your data so that only authorized parties can read it. Encryption is especially critical for mobile devices since they are easily lost or stolen. Device-level encryption is available on both iOS and Android devices.

Mobile App Security

Mobile apps are another area of concern when it comes to mobile security. Apps may contain vulnerabilities that can be exploited by cybercriminals, which could give them access to sensitive information. There are a few best practices that developers and users alike should follow to ensure that mobile apps are secure:

❖ Conduct threat modelling: Developers should conduct thorough threat modelling to identify possible attack vectors and vulnerabilities that their apps may face.

❖ Secure coding: Developers should use secure coding practices to prevent possible exploits and vulnerabilities.

❖   App store reviews: Users should only download apps from trusted app stores such as the Apple App Store or Google Play, which employ security measures such as code scanning and app review procedures to ensure that apps are safe.

❖   User awareness: Users should be aware of app permissions and only grant necessary permissions to apps. Additionally, users should avoid jailbreaking or rooting their devices, which can disable essential security features.

Bring Your Own Device (BYOD) Policies

Employers are increasingly allowing employees to use their own personal mobile devices for work purposes, which is known as Bring Your Own Device (BYOD). While BYOD offers numerous benefits such as increased productivity and cost savings, it also poses significant security challenges, as employees may use unsecured devices or install insecure apps onto company networks. To mitigate these risks, businesses can develop BYOD policies, which should include:

❖   Mobile device management: The use of an MDM platform can allow businesses to monitor and control access to company data on employee devices.

❖   Employee education: Employees should be trained in proper mobile security practices, such as using strong passwords, avoiding public Wi-Fi networks, and keeping devices updated with the latest software.

❖   App permissions: Employees should be informed of the risks that come with downloading certain apps and should only download trusted apps from reputable sources.

Mobile Device Tracking and Theft Prevention

Mobile device tracking is another important security measure for mobile devices. Both iOS and Android offer built-in tracking features that allow users to remotely locate and lock their devices if they are lost or stolen. To prevent theft, users can take measures such as keeping their mobile devices secure by using passwords, keeping their devices close in public areas, and avoiding leaving them unattended in vehicles.

Mobile Network Security

Mobile network security is another key factor in overall mobile device security. There are several ways to secure mobile network connections, such as using secure passwords and two-factor authentication, avoiding public Wi-Fi networks, and using VPNs to encrypt data traffic.

Conclusion

Mobile device security is a complex and rapidly evolving field, with new threats emerging all the time. By remaining vigilant and following best practices such as encrypting data, securing devices, and closely monitoring mobile app usage, individuals and businesses can protect themselves from mobile security threats and ensure that their data and devices remain secure.

CHAPTER 9: CLOUD SECURITY

In recent years, cloud computing has become an integral part of business operations, offering immense advantages in terms of scalability, cost savings, and flexibility. With distributed computing resources, businesses can easily access shared IT resources, store data and applications in virtual servers, and collaborate seamlessly with their partners and customers across different geographic locations. However, cloud computing also poses unique security challenges and risks that need careful attention and management. In this chapter, we will explore the key concepts and practices of cloud security, including cloud models, security standards and compliance, access controls, encryption, data loss prevention (DLP), and monitoring.

Cloud Computing Models

Cloud computing refers to the practice of using remote servers and networks to store, manage, and process data, instead of using local servers and devices. Cloud services are usually offered by third-party providers, who provide the infrastructure, platform, software, and security controls needed to host and manage business applications and data. There are three main cloud computing models that businesses can choose from, depending on their needs and resources:

❖ Infrastructure as a service (IaaS) - In this model, businesses can rent computing resources, such as virtual servers, storage devices, and security tools, from a cloud provider. This allows businesses to avoid the costs and complexity of managing their own on-premise infrastructure, while retaining full control over their virtual servers and applications.

❖ Platform as a service (PaaS) - In this model, businesses can use a cloud provider's platform and development tools to build and deploy their own applications and services. This allows businesses to focus on their core application logic, while leaving the underlying infrastructure and security to the cloud provider.

❖ Software as a service (SaaS) - In this model, businesses can use a cloud provider's software applications, such as email, CRM, HR, and accounting tools, without having to install or maintain them on their own devices. This allows businesses to access the latest software features and updates, while minimizing the costs and risks of software licensing and management.

Advantages and Disadvantages of Cloud Computing

Cloud computing offers numerous advantages over traditional on-premise computing, including:

❖ Scalability and flexibility: Cloud services can be quickly scaled up or down, depending on business needs and user demand. This allows businesses to avoid over-provisioning or under-utilization of their IT resources, and to adapt to changing market conditions and growth opportunities.

❖ Cost savings: Cloud services can often be more cost-effective than on-premise infrastructure, as they eliminate the need for businesses to purchase and manage their own hardware, software, and maintenance. Cloud providers can also leverage economies of scale to offer lower prices and better features than individual businesses can achieve on their own.

❖ Accessibility and collaboration: Cloud services can be accessed from anywhere, as long as there is an internet connection. This allows businesses to work remotely, to collaborate with partners and customers across different locations and time zones, and to share data and applications securely.

However, cloud computing also poses certain disadvantages and risks that businesses need to be aware of, such as:

❖ Security and privacy risks: Cloud services are accessed over the internet, which increases the risk of cyber-attacks, data breaches, and unauthorized access. Cloud providers may also store data and applications in multiple locations, which can create regulatory compliance challenges and data residency issues.

❖ Availability and performance risks: Cloud services depend on reliable internet connectivity and server uptime, which can be affected by network outages, equipment failures, and natural disasters. Cloud providers may also impose limits or restrictions on bandwidth, storage, and processing capacity, which can affect application performance and user experience.

❖ Governance and control risks: Cloud services may require businesses to relinquish some degree of governance and control over their data and applications, as they rely on third-party providers to manage their cloud infrastructure and security controls. This can create challenges in terms of regulatory compliance, auditability, and data sovereignty.

Cloud Security and Compliance Standards

To mitigate the security and compliance risks of cloud computing, various standards and frameworks have been developed to guide businesses and cloud providers in implementing best practices and controls. Some of the most commonly used cloud security standards and regulations include:

❖ ISO 27001: This is an internationally recognized standard for information security management systems (ISMS), which provides a framework for managing and protecting sensitive information assets. ISO 27001 covers key areas of cloud security, such as access controls, data protection, incident management, and risk assessments.

❖ SOC 2: This is a set of auditing standards developed by the American Institute of Certified Public Accountants (AICPA), which focuses on cloud service organizations (CSOs) that provide SaaS, IaaS, and PaaS services. SOC 2 covers key areas of cloud security, such as infrastructure security, data privacy, availability, and processing integrity.

❖ HIPAA: This is a U.S. federal regulation that establishes security and privacy standards for protected health information (PHI), which includes medical records, payment data, and other sensitive healthcare information. HIPAA requires businesses and cloud providers to implement security controls that protect PHI against unauthorized access, disclosure, and alteration.

❖ GDPR: This is a European Union regulation that governs the processing, storage, and sharing of personal data, which includes names, addresses, email addresses, and sensitive personal information, across all industries. GDPR requires businesses and cloud providers to provide transparency, accountability, and user consent in handling personal data, and to implement security controls that protect personal data against unauthorized access, disclosure, and loss.

Shared Responsibility Model in Cloud Computing

One of the unique features of cloud computing is the shared responsibility model, which delineates the security responsibilities of businesses and cloud providers. Under this model, cloud providers are responsible for securing the underlying infrastructure and platform of their cloud services, such as physical security, network security, and host security. Businesses are responsible for securing their own data and applications that are stored and processed on the cloud services, such as data encryption, access controls, and user authentication. The exact division of security responsibilities depends on the specific type of cloud service and the cloud provider's policies and procedures.

Access Controls and Identity Management

Access controls and identity management are critical components of cloud security, as they ensure that only authorized users and devices can access cloud services and data. Access controls refer to the policies, techniques, and tools that restrict or permit access to cloud resources, based on user roles, permissions, and authentication factors. Identity management refers to the processes and tools that manage user identities and attributes, such as usernames, passwords, biometrics, and certificates, across multiple cloud services and platforms.

Some of the best practices and tools for access controls and identity management in cloud computing include:

> Role-based access control (RBAC): This is a method of access control that grants permissions based on a user's role within an organization, such as administrator, manager, or employee. RBAC ensures that users have the appropriate level of access to cloud resources, based on their job responsibilities and authorized tasks.

> Multi-factor authentication (MFA): This is a method of user authentication that requires two or more factors of

authentication, such as a password, a security token, or a fingerprint scan, to access cloud resources. MFA enhances the security of cloud services by reducing the risk of unauthorized access through stolen or guessed passwords.

➢ Access control lists (ACLs): This is a method of access control that defines a list of permissions for specific users or groups of users, based on their IP addresses, time of access, or other criteria. ACLs allow businesses to fine-tune their access controls for specific cloud resources, based on the level of sensitivity and risk associated with each resource.

➢ Single sign-on (SSO): This is a method of user authentication that enables users to access multiple cloud services and platforms with a single set of credentials, instead of having to remember separate usernames and passwords for each service. SSO improves user productivity, while reducing the security risks associated with password reuse and exposure.

Encryption in the Cloud

Encryption is a key method of protecting sensitive data in the cloud, as it ensures that data is scrambled and unreadable to unauthorized users or devices. Encryption can be applied to data at rest, which refers to data that is stored in databases, file systems, or backups, and data in transit, which refers to data that is transmitted between devices and servers over the internet. Some of the best practices and tools for encryption in the cloud include:

❖ Key management: This is a set of policies and techniques that ensure the secure generation, storage, and distribution of encryption keys, which are used to encrypt and decrypt data. Key management can be done by the cloud provider, the business, or a third-party key management service.

❖ Data masking: This is a technique that replaces sensitive

data with fake or scrambled data, while preserving the format and structure of the original data. Data masking can be used to protect sensitive data, such as credit card numbers, social security numbers, and health records, from unauthorized access or disclosure.

❖ Transport Layer Security (TLS): This is a protocol that encrypts data in transit between devices and servers, using public key cryptography. TLS is widely used to secure web traffic, email, and other internet applications that rely on secure connections.

❖ Data encryption standard (DES): This is an encryption algorithm that uses a 56-bit key to encrypt and decrypt data. DES is commonly used in legacy systems and applications but is considered less secure than more advanced encryption algorithms, such as Advanced Encryption Standard (AES).

Data Loss Prevention (DLP) in the Cloud

Data loss prevention (DLP) refers to the policies, techniques, and tools that prevent sensitive data from being lost, leaked, or stolen from cloud services. DLP can be applied to data at rest, in motion, or in use, and can be used to enforce data retention policies, detect data breaches or insider threats, and monitor data activity logs. Some of the best practices and tools for DLP in the cloud include:

CHAPTER 10: SOCIAL MEDIA SECURITY

Social media platforms, such as Facebook, Twitter, Instagram, and LinkedIn, have become an integral part of our personal and professional lives. While these platforms offer benefits such as staying connected with friends and colleagues, networking opportunities, and promoting businesses, they also come with their own set of security risks. In this chapter, we will discuss these risks and the steps you can take to ensure social media security.

Risks and Benefits of Social Media Use

The most significant risk associated with social media use is the loss of personal information and online privacy. When you create a profile on social media, you are sharing a wealth of information about yourself. This information includes your name, age, location, job, interests, photos, and more. Unfortunately, this information can be used by cybercriminals to create phishing scams or to launch social engineering attacks.

Phishing and Identity Theft

Phishing is a scam in which an attacker sends a message that appears to be from a trustworthy source, such as a social media platform, bank, or government agency, to trick users into revealing sensitive information, such as login credentials or credit card details. Phishing can also result in identity theft, in which an attacker uses personal information to open fraudulent accounts or to make purchases.

Phishing attacks can take various forms, including spear-phishing, whaling, and smishing. Spear-phishing is a targeted attack in which the attacker sends a message tailored to a particular user or organization. Whaling is a type of spear-phishing that specifically targets high-profile individuals, such as CEOs or politicians. Smishing is a type of phishing that occurs via SMS or text message.

Impact on Personal and Professional Reputation

In addition to online privacy concerns, social media use can also impact personal and professional reputation. Social media posts and comments can be taken out of context or misinterpreted, resulting in negative consequences such as job loss or damage to personal relationships.

For businesses, social media use can have serious reputational consequences if employees post inappropriate or controversial content on behalf of the company. The rise of cancel culture means that any negative attention on social media can have significant financial and reputational implications for an organization.

Social Media Policies and Guidelines for Businesses

To mitigate social media risks, it is essential for businesses to establish and enforce social media policies and guidelines. These policies should outline acceptable use of social media, prohibit harassment and discrimination, and provide guidance on privacy settings.

Furthermore, businesses should conduct employee training on social media use and the potential risks associated with it. This training can include phishing awareness, password management, and best practices for posting content online. It is also essential for businesses to monitor social media activity for potential threats or reputational damage.

Promoting Social Media Security Awareness

Individuals can take several steps to promote social media security awareness, including:

➤ Using strong passwords and two-factor authentication (2FA) to protect their accounts from unauthorized access.

➤ Limiting the amount of personal information shared on social media profiles.

➤ Understanding the potential risks associated with social media use and being aware of common social engineering tactics.

➤ Being cautious of unsolicited messages and friend requests, especially from unknown or suspicious accounts.

➤ Regularly reviewing and updating privacy settings on social media accounts.

➤ Avoiding posting sensitive or personally identifiable information on social media networks.

Monitoring and Reporting Social Media Threats

Finally, it is important to monitor social media activity for potential threats and to report any suspicious activity to the appropriate authorities. This reporting may include cyberbullying, harassment, or phishing attempts.

In conclusion, social media use is highly prevalent in today's society, and it is essential to be aware of the potential risks associated with it. Implementing strong social media security practices, both on a personal and business level, is crucial to protecting personal information and maintaining a positive reputation. By following the steps outlined in this chapter, you can enjoy the benefits of social media while mitigating the associated risks.

CHAPTER 11:
INTERNET OF THINGS
(IOT) SECURITY

The Internet of Things (IoT) is the network of physical devices, vehicles, home appliances, and other items embedded with electronics, software, sensors, and connectivity which enables these objects to connect and exchange data. With the growth of IoT, there are security concerns with the increasing use of these devices in our daily lives. This chapter focuses on exploring the security risks and measures to ensure security when using IoT devices for individuals and businesses.

IoT devices and their functions

IoT devices vary in shapes and sizes, and their functions range from simple household appliances, such as smart fridges and thermostats, to industrial machinery, with sensors for measuring performance, temperature, and other variables. Other uses of IoT include vehicle tracking, environmental monitoring, health monitoring, and home automation systems. The range of devices that people use gives a hint of the security risks since they all communicate with other connected devices, which creates a vector of attack for hackers.

IoT security risks and threats

There are three main types of IoT security threats, which include:

1. Privacy risk - IoT devices collect and transmit a large amount of data. This data can include sensitive information, such as passwords, email addresses, and credit card details. Hackers can gain access to this information and breach the privacy of the users.

2. Operational risk - Devices can get breached through malware and viruses that can cause malfunctions in the device. This can lead to physical harm, as in the case of medical devices.

3. Physical risk - Attacks on IoT devices can create physical harm, such as in the case of self-driving cars. A breach in the car's security system could lead to injuries or fatalities.

IoT security standards and regulations

Many organizations have established security standards for IoT devices, including the International Organisation for Standardization (ISO), the Institute of Electrical and Electronics Engineers (IEEE), and the National Institute of Standards and Technology (NIST). However, as the industry continues to grow, new vulnerabilities may arise, and these standards may become outdated. There is, therefore, a need for constant reviews and updates to ensure that the standards remain relevant to the current IoT security environment.

Network segmentation and isolation for IoT devices

IoT devices ought to be segmented into their own network to prevent hackers from accessing critical enterprise systems if one IoT device gets breached. If users must connect the IoT devices to the organization's main network, the organization should ensure that access controls limit the devices' capabilities to the lowest level necessary for its intended purpose.

Secure coding and firmware updates for IoT devices

Developers should also take measures to ensure that the codes for developing IoT devices are secure. The devices should be more than mere 'plug-and-play' since hackers look for vulnerabilities in default settings that can be easily exploited. IoT manufacturers should continually release firmware updates to patch security vulnerabilities discovered.

Encryption and authentication for IoT devices

IoT manufacturers should include strong encryption and authentication protocols in their devices to ensure that the data transmitted from the device is secure. Using outdated encryption methods or weak authentication protocols can lead to hackers breaching the system.

IoT data privacy and protection

IoT devices often collect large amounts of data, and this data must be secure to prevent breaches. Users should have control over their data and know how their information is being used. The data should be encrypted during transmission and at rest in storage. IoT manufacturers should also provide clear data retention policies.

Managing IoT security for businesses

IoT devices can help increase efficiency and productivity, but there are risks involved. Therefore, businesses that have embraced IoT devices should undertake a thorough risk assessment to identify potential IoT vulnerabilities and impacts. The organization should also create an incident response plan to minimize cybersecurity risks; this should include testing, isolation, preservation, and analysis of data in case of a breach.

Conclusion

In conclusion, IoT provides endless possibilities for businesses and individuals alike. However, with the significant number of connected devices, the ongoing development of the technology, and hackers incessantly improving their tactics, it becomes imperative that the manufacturers and users alike take the necessary precautions to ensure the security of the devices. The principles discussed in this chapter provide a foundation for creating and implementing security standards that can be applied to IoT systems to create a secure infrastructure.

CHAPTER 12:
INCIDENT RESPONSE
AND RECOVERY

Incidents happen. And when it comes to computer security, incidents can be particularly severe. Unplanned network downtime, data breaches, viruses, and ransomware are but a few of the adversities that can take place. Devices, networks, and systems may all fail – even in the best security environments.

Because of this, the development of an incident response plan is critical. This plan should be a set of comprehensive instructions on what to do when an incident occurs - as speed is of the essence - with special emphasis on the restoration of affected systems.

The importance of incident response planning

In terms of computer security, the adage "an ounce of prevention is worth a pound of cure" rings true. However, since no system is foolproof, organizations must also put in place a plan that clearly details how they intend to respond to an attack. A clear and concise incident response plan is critical for ensuring that any potential damage is as limited as it can be.

Implementing an incident response plan promotes the following outcomes:

➢ It promotes the early detection of an incident.

➤ Ensures the prompt containment of the incident.

➤ It minimizes the adverse effects of an incident.

➤ It ensures the prompt restoration of the normal working environment.

➤ It minimizes the number of incidents that take place.

The importance of incident response cannot be overstated. By having an established response team, you can minimize the damage caused by a breach and ensure the swift recovery of lost data.

Incident response team roles and responsibilities

The role of an incident response team is to organize and coordinate the response to an incident in line with the established response plan. This team should consist of personnel that possess the necessary skills and expertise to detect, contain, and recover from cyberattacks.

Typically, team members include a team leader, a spokesperson, representatives from law enforcement agencies, technical staff, network administrators, security professionals, and legal advisors. Sound judgement and responsibility are two vital traits required from each individual on the team.

The following are the general roles and responsibilities of each member of the incident response team:

❖ Team Leader: Leaders must have experience in IT infrastructure and ensure team members understand their responsibilities and deliverables. Leaders are responsible for ensuring that the incident response plan is current, and operations are smooth, timely, and effective.

❖ Spokesperson: This role requires a professional with excellent communication skills and experience in dealing with the media and public relations. A spokesperson's responsibilities include communicating with customers, the media, and other stakeholders on behalf of the organization.

❖ Legal Advisors: Incident response teams must have access to legal experts to provide guidance on privacy and data protection laws. They should also be able to provide advice on possible legal repercussions that the organization may face as a result of the incident.

❖ Technical Staff: Technical staff plays a critical role in collecting artifacts from affected systems and providing expert analysis of the details in an incident. They must also assist in creating and testing response procedures and recommend mitigation techniques.

❖ Network Administrators: Network administrators are responsible for monitoring networks and logs continuously, identifying and responding to incidents, updating domain names, and blocking unnecessary traffic from malicious sites or IP addresses.

❖ Security Professionals: These personnel are the front line. They have the confidential knowledge and tools to determine an attacker's objectives and natures. They are responsible for identifying the entry point of the attack, system vulnerabilities, and recommend remedial actions.

(Note - Sometimes, an organization may not have the capacity to form an internal incident response team, especially small-to-medium-sized companies. In such cases, contracting third-party cyber incident response companies may be appropriate.)

Incident response procedures and protocols

The incident response plan should include procedures for

immediate response to an incident, incident containment, data recovery and restoration, and incident follow-up.

Immediate Response procedures should include:

❖ Incident detection: It is crucial to conduct a thorough investigation of the incident to determine its nature, severity, and scope.

❖ Incident categorization: You must categorize incidents based on their nature, such as virus threats, application attacks, or unauthorized access.

❖ Incident analysis: Analysis is required to determine the possible risks associated with the incident.

❖ Information gathering: Teams must gather information such as the type, source, and timestamp of data, as well as details on affected hardware and applications.

❖ Action plan creation: Action plans include how to contain, mitigate, and restore system operations.

Incident containment procedures should include:

❖ Isolation of affected systems to prevent further damage.

❖ Identification of the source or attacker responsible for the incident.

❖ Implementation of stop-gap measures to prevent further damage or prevent further unauthorized activities.

❖ Establish a response team that consists of skilled professionals with technical knowledge and experience.

Data recovery and restoration procedures should include:

➢ Restoration of damaged data and/or compromised systems

➤ Data validation on the integrity of backup data

Incident follow-up procedures should include:

➤ An evaluation of the overall damage of the compromised system.

➤ Updating the incident response plan

➤ Incorporating lessons learned.

➤ Refining procedures to prevent similar incidents in the future.

Incident detection and escalation

Incident detection and escalation go hand-in-hand. Early detection of attacks is crucial and can significantly mitigate the adverse effects of an incident. Any indication of a security breach, such as messages, system alerts, or reports, should be immediately assessed.

Once an incident has been detected, escalation to the organization's incident response team must commence.

Ideally, the response team uses the organization's various monitoring systems to obtain an incident report that contains detailed information on the nature, extent, and repercussions of the breach.

The team must also implement the organization's cascading response criteria and procedures. During an escalation action, the team must ensure to:

❖ Identify the incident classification, which will determine the level of priority action.

❖ Identify the action required, such as data removal, isolation, and equipment closure.

❖ Map or configure access points or controls that the attacker or threat actor may have accessed or removed while executing the incident.

❖ Provide updated incident reports to senior management for approval.

Containment and eradication of incidents

After an incident has been verified, the incident response team, led by the team leader, must ensure containment and provide swift response actions. During incident containment and eradication, the following actions may be taken:

➤ Isolation of the victim system to prevent further damage to the system, network, database, and application.

➤ Isolating vulnerable endpoints to exclude further attack from affected servers, gadgets, or network links.

➤ Blocking the attacker's access path inside the system, network, or database.

➤ Obtaining a backup system to restore affected data and alternative resources during disaster recovery.

Forensic Analysis of incidents

Forensic analysis of incidents is critical, and it usually occurs after the containment and eradication of all potential threats. Forensic analysis goes beyond merely containing the incident and ascertains the nature and purpose of the attack. During forensic analysis, the team gathers and processes digital evidence for use in investigations and legal proceedings.

Communication and reporting during an incident

During the incident response process, all stakeholders must be kept aware of the situation. Communication is key, and because uncontrolled communication can create chaos, communication during an incident must be managed cautiously.

The incident response team should develop and implement a communication plan for informing all stakeholders, who include customers, senior management, business units, third-party partners, and external regulatory bodies. As the incident evolves, team members must communicate constantly to keep senior management informed about the incident's severity and required actions in its mitigation and eradication.

Post-incident Review and improvement

Once the incident has been resolved, the organization must review the incident response plan. This review will enable the response team to assess the incident and make necessary improvements to prevent similar incidents in the future.

During post-incident review, teams must:

❖ Review the effectiveness of the incident response plan

❖   Determine the proactive security controls to minimize similar incidents.

❖   Ensure predefined metrics are established to assess the efficacy of an incident response plan.

❖   Refine the incident response plan and incorporate lessons learned.

Conclusion

Computer security incidents happen, and the scale of damage caused can be significant. At times like these, having a well-drilled incident response team that's well-versed in the response plan is critical. Collaboration, communication, and coordination between incident response teams and other stakeholders can help ensure timely response and recovery from an attack. Regular training, audit, and test plans are critical in ensuring the team remains knowledgeable and updated on the company's business environment and threat landscape. For corporations, investing in incident response can save significant costs on both operational recovery and reputational management.

CHAPTER 13: RISK MANAGEMENT AND COMPLIANCE

Risk management is an essential aspect of computer security. It involves the identification, assessment, and mitigation of risks to the confidentiality, integrity, and availability of computer systems and data. This chapter will explore the principles of risk management and the various frameworks and regulations that help organizations ensure compliance with legal and regulatory requirements.

Principles of Risk Management

Risk management is a process that involves the following steps:

Step 1: Risk identification: The first step in the risk management process is to identify potential risks that could impact the organization. This includes both internal and external risks, such as software vulnerabilities, employee errors, natural disasters, and cyberattacks.

Step 2: Risk assessment: Once potential risks have been identified, they must be assessed to determine their likelihood and potential impact. This includes analysing the probability of a risk occurring, and the potential consequences if it does.

Step 3: Risk mitigation: Once the risks have been identified and assessed, measures can be taken to mitigate them. This could include implementing security controls, developing incident response plans, or transferring the risk through insurance.

Step 4: Risk monitoring: The risk management process is ongoing, and risks must be continuously monitored to ensure that security measures remain effective. This includes analysing the effectiveness of security controls, tracking critical assets, and staying informed about emerging threats and vulnerabilities.

Risk Assessment and Analysis Techniques

Risk assessment and analysis techniques help organizations identify and prioritize risks so that they can be effectively mitigated. Some common risk assessment techniques include:

➢　　　Asset-based risk assessment: This approach involves identifying and prioritizing assets based on their importance to the organization and the potential impact of a security breach.

➢　　　Threat-based risk assessment: This approach involves identifying potential threats and vulnerabilities and assessing the likelihood and potential impact of those threats.

➢　　 Vulnerability-based risk assessment: This approach involves identifying system vulnerabilities and assessing the potential impact of an exploit.

➢　　 Quantitative risk assessment: This involves assigning numeric values to the probability and impact of a security event and using this data to prioritize risks.

➢　　 Qualitative risk assessment: This involves assessing risks based on subjective factors such as expert judgment, organizational culture, and corporate values.

Risk Mitigation and Avoidance Strategies

There are several strategies that organizations can use to minimize their exposure to risk:

❖ Risk avoidance: This involves eliminating or reducing the activity that poses a risk. For example, an organization could avoid storing sensitive data on mobile devices to reduce the risk of data breaches.

❖ Risk reduction: This involves implementing security controls to minimize the likelihood or impact of a risk. For example, an organization could implement intrusion detection and prevention systems to reduce the risk of cyberattacks.

❖ Risk transfer: This involves transferring the risk to another party, such as an insurance company. For example, an organization could purchase cyber insurance to help offset the costs of a security breach.

❖ Risk acceptance: This involves accepting and living with the risk. For example, an organization might decide that the cost of implementing security controls outweighs the potential impact of a security breach.

Compliance Frameworks and Regulations

There are many compliance frameworks and regulations that organizations must adhere to in order to ensure the confidentiality, integrity, and availability of their systems and data. Some common frameworks and regulations include:

❖ Payment Card Industry Data Security Standard (PCI DSS): This framework applies to organizations that handle credit card payments and requires them to implement specific security controls to protect cardholder data.

❖ Health Insurance Portability and Accountability Act (HIPAA): This regulation applies to organizations that handle medical records and requires them to implement specific security controls to protect patient data.

❖ National Institute of Standards and Technology (NIST) Cybersecurity Framework: This framework provides a set of guidelines and best practices for managing and reducing cyber risk.

❖ General Data Protection Regulation (GDPR): This regulation applies to organizations operating within the European Union and requires them to implement specific security controls to protect personal data.

❖ Sarbanes-Oxley Act (SOX): This regulation applies to publicly traded companies and requires them to implement specific security controls to protect financial data.

Risk Management for Outsourcing and Third-Party Vendors

In today's interconnected business environment, many organizations rely on outsourcing and third-party vendors for critical business functions. However, this also introduces additional security risks. Organizations must take steps to ensure that their vendors and partners are also adhering to security best practices and compliance regulations.

To manage these risks, organizations should implement the following practices:

❖ Vendor risk assessments: Before partnering with a new vendor, organizations should conduct a thorough risk assessment to identify potential risks and ensure that the vendor is complying with security best practices.

❖ Contractual safeguards: Organizations should include security requirements in their contracts with vendors and partners. These requirements should specify the security controls that the vendor must implement and should establish consequences for noncompliance.

❖   Ongoing monitoring: Organizations must continuously monitor their vendors and partners to ensure that they are adhering to security best practices. This includes regular audits and security assessments.

❖   Incident response planning: Organizations should develop incident response plans that include their vendors and partners. In the event of a security incident, the vendor's response should be aligned with the organization's response to minimize the impact.

Conclusion

Effective risk management is critical to ensuring the security and integrity of computer systems and data. By identifying potential risks, assessing their likelihood and impact, and implementing measures to mitigate them, organizations can reduce their exposure to security breaches and other threats. Compliance frameworks and regulations provide a set of guidelines and best practices for managing and reducing cyber risk, while the practices outlined for managing third-party risks and vendors ensure that organizations are protected from unintended vulnerabilities. By prioritizing risk management, organizations can ensure that their computer systems are secure and protected.

CHAPTER 14:
SECURITY CULTURE

In previous chapters, we have discussed in-depth the various threats and vulnerabilities that exist in the realm of computer security, as well as the measures that can be taken to mitigate and prevent them. However, none of these measures can be truly effective unless there exists a culture of security within an organization.

A security-conscious culture is one where everyone knows and understands the importance of good security practices and takes an active role in maintaining it. This chapter will explore the key elements involved in fostering a security culture, what motivates people to maintain good security practices, and how organizations can incentivize and encourage their employees to do so.

Establishing a Security-Conscious Culture

Creating a security-conscious culture starts from the top down. Leaders and managers within an organization must recognize the importance of security and the risks associated with not prioritizing it. They must prioritize the development and maintenance of security policies and procedures, as well as ensure that they are regularly updated and enforced.

Alongside security policies and procedures, a security-conscious culture can also be fostered through investment in employee education and awareness programs. Such programs aim to educate employees on the importance of security practices, common threats and attacks, and how they can maintain good security practices, both in the workplace and at home. These programs can take various forms, including seminars, training sessions, and online courses.

Encouraging Reporting of Security Incidents and Near-Misses

Another critical factor in developing a security-conscious culture is the establishment of an environment where employees can freely report security incidents and near-misses without fear of repercussions. It may be tempting to punish employees who make mistakes; however, this creates a culture where employees are hesitant to report issues, even if doing so would benefit the organization as a whole. When a culture exists where employees feel comfortable in reporting issues, it is easier to identify areas of weakness and to address them quickly and efficiently.

Promoting Security Awareness through Incentives and Recognition

Incentives and recognition programs can also be an effective tool in promoting security awareness and fostering a security-conscious culture. Many organizations hold regular security competitions, where employees are incentivized to identify potential security flaws or make suggestions for improving security. The goal of these competitions is to encourage employees to be proactive in identifying potential security issues and develop a culture of continuous security improvement.

Creating Security Policies and Procedures

Security policies and procedures serve as the backbone of any security-conscious culture. They describe the protocols and standards for maintaining security within the organization, as well as the responsibilities of employees and management in the event of a security incident. Good security policies and procedures will address all areas of potential security risk, as well as preventative measures for minimizing such risk.

The creation of security policies and procedures must go hand in hand with employee education and training. It is essential to ensure that employees understand company security policies and procedures, and the role they play in maintaining good security practices.

Social Engineering Tests and Phishing Simulations

Social engineering tests and phishing simulations can be a powerful tool in promoting security awareness and testing employee knowledge of company security policies and procedures. These simulations help employees to identify potentially suspicious emails, texts, and other forms of communication and can prevent them from instinctively clicking on potential threats. Security-conscious cultures must be proactive in testing employee knowledge to help identify and address potential areas of weakness.

Celebrating Successes in Security

Celebrating successes in security can be an effective way of cementing a security-conscious culture. When security incidents are prevented through the actions of employees who have demonstrated good security practices, their contributions should be recognized. Recognizing such contributions publicly or with incentives can not only encourage further good practices but also incentivizes others to emulate them.

Fostering a Culture of Continuous Improvement

Finally, it is essential to understand that developing a security-conscious culture is not a one-time achievement but rather an ongoing process of continuous improvement. Threats and vulnerabilities evolve, and thus it is necessary to regularly reassess existing security policies and procedures, as well as ensure that employees are adequately educated on current best practices. Organizations that foster a culture of continuous improvement and aim to stay ahead of emerging threats are better positioned to mitigate potential incidents and protect their systems and data.

Conclusion

Developing a security-conscious culture is more than just implementing robust security policies and procedures. It requires investment in employee education, incentives and recognition programs, active testing, as well as leadership that prioritizes the importance of security. When organizations invest the time and resources necessary to develop a security-conscious culture, they can better safeguard their systems and data and build a stronger system of defence against the ever-evolving landscape of security threats.

CHAPTER 15: EMERGING TRENDS IN COMPUTER SECURITY

As the world becomes increasingly reliant on technology, the importance of computer security cannot be overstated. As new technologies emerge, so do new security threats and vulnerabilities. In this chapter, we will examine emerging trends in computer security that are shaping the future of this field.

Artificial Intelligence (AI) and Machine Learning (ML) in Security

Artificial intelligence and machine learning are transforming computer security in various ways, such as identifying and mitigating security threats in real-time. AI and ML algorithms can detect threats that may be too complex for humans to identify and can reduce response times.

However, these technologies also require a significant amount of data to operate effectively, which can potentially lead to privacy concerns. Additionally, attackers may also use AI and ML to launch smarter attacks, so it is important that researchers continue to study and develop better security measures incorporating these technologies.

Blockchain and Cryptocurrency Security

Blockchain technology and cryptocurrencies are becoming increasingly popular, yet they also present new security challenges. Cryptocurrencies, for example, are vulnerable to hackers who can steal or manipulate them. The nature of blockchain technology means that any transaction is publicly visible, however, that can hinder individual privacy.

As blockchain and cryptocurrencies continue to grow in popularity, more attention will be paid to security considerations. Developers will need to focus on building more robust security systems that address the specific vulnerabilities of these technologies.

Quantum Computing and its Impact on Cryptography

Quantum computing is a new and powerful form of computing, which has the potential to break current encryption algorithms, which are the backbone of modern-day cryptography. Quantum computers operate using quantum bits, or qubits, which can work on multiple calculations simultaneously.

If quantum computing technology progresses, it could render current encryption algorithms insecure, leading to the development of new algorithms that can resist quantum computing attacks. However, there are also opportunities for improvements in cryptography using quantum computing, which can lead to the development of more efficient and secure encryption algorithms for the future.

Internet Censorship and Surveillance

Internet censorship and surveillance by governments has become a major issue in recent years. From the collection of personal information by tech companies, to government surveillance programs, the threat to online privacy is greater than ever before. As technologies develop, the ability to monitor individuals online activities will only grow.

In the future, it is important that people advocate for their basic rights to privacy, and work together to implement frameworks and measures that ensure individuals can continue to enjoy their rights within the digital realm.

Cybersecurity Workforce Shortage and Diversity

With the rapidly increasing demand for cybersecurity professionals, there is a significant shortage in the numbers of qualified and experienced professionals in the field. This shortage also extends to diverse representation within the industry, including the underrepresentation of women and other marginalized groups.

To overcome this shortage, educational programs must continue to promote sophisticated computer security knowledge at a fundamental level to the next generation of cybersecurity workers. To address diversity problems, organizations should make committed efforts to employ or train employees from underrepresented groups.

Augmented and Virtual Reality (AR/VR) Security Risks

The rise of AR/VR technologies, like Oculus Rift, HoloLens and other emerging technologies guarantees unprecedented opportunities for various applications. However, these technologies also pose new security risks like those associated with using internet-connected devices.

From the point of privacy issues using AR/VR applications to deliberate attacks against AR/VR vulnerabilities, various security risks are now emerging from AR/VR applications. To eliminate these risks, developers must focus on developing automated controls to prevent attacks and unauthorized access.

Biometric Authentication and Privacy Concerns

Biometric authentication technology, such as fingerprint or facial recognition, is becoming increasingly popular as an alternative to traditional password authentication. Its increased use, however, raises the risk that this technology may be used in malicious ways, such as surveillance or hacking.

To address privacy concerns, developers need to build more secure systems that respect individual privacy. It is important that any biometric data is securely stored and cannot be accessed without proper authorization.

The Future of Computer Security Research and Development

The computer security field has experienced significant growth in recent years. In the future, we expect it to only become more important. The next step in computer security is moving toward proactive security measures, rather than reactive measures. In the future, the focus will be on building systems that are fully secured from the outset, rather than attempting to shore up vulnerabilities after they have been exploited.

In conclusion, the rapid advancements in technology are resulting in new and innovative opportunities, but with them come new security risks. Threats that were once seen as insurmountable are now being supported by technological advancements. Cybersecurity professionals are working tirelessly to keep up with these emerging threats and trends, aiming to build more secure systems and solutions to protect the individual and companies against these new risks in the near and far future.

CHAPTER 16: USING OPEN SOURCE TOOLS FOR COMPUTER SECURITY

Introduction to open source security tools

In this chapter, we will explore open source tools that computer security professionals can use to monitor, detect, and mitigate potential security risks. Open source tools have become an increasingly popular option among technology professionals due to their flexibility, cost-effectiveness, and the ability to tailor to specific needs. Here are some of the most commonly used open source security tools:

Network analysis and monitoring tools:

❖ Wireshark: This is a popular open source tool used for network analysis and troubleshooting. It captures live network traffic and allows users to analyse it in real-time.

❖ Nmap: This is a network exploration and auditing tool. Its primary use is to scan systems and networks to identify open ports, identify services on those ports, and assess vulnerability risks.

❖ Tcpdump: This tool captures and analyses packets on

a network. Tcpdump can identify targeted packets on a network that may indicate an intrusion attempt or other security breach.

Vulnerability scanners and exploit frameworks:

❖ Metasploit: This is an open source framework that offers a comprehensive database of exploits and vulnerability information. It enables users to test their system's security and identify potential vulnerabilities.

❖ OpenVAS: This is a vulnerability scanner used to identify security risks on a network. OpenVAS enables users to identify and rate levels of security risks and prioritize necessary mitigation measures.

❖ Nikto: This is an open source web server scanner that looks for vulnerabilities in web servers and reports any detected risks to the user.

Password cracking and auditing tools:

❖ John the Ripper: This is a password cracking tool used to identify weak passwords. It works by decrypting password hashes and attempting to identify the corresponding password.

❖ Hashcat: This is a hash cracking tool that uses brute-force attacks to guess or uncover passwords. It can identify passwords stored in cryptographic hashes.

❖ Cain and Abel: This is a password recovery tool that can extract and decrypt passwords from Windows systems. It can recover passwords that have been lost or forgotten.

Encryption and hashing tools:

❖ GnuPG: This is an open source encryption tool that can be

used for both messages and files. It enables users to encrypt sensitive information and secure communications.

❖ OpenSSL: This is an open source tool used for the creation, management, and certification of SSL/TLS connections. It helps to secure communication between servers and clients.

❖ HashTools: This is a hashing tool that encrypts or validates data. It can be used to create and check file checksums, providing assurance that the file has not been tampered with.

Incident response and forensics tools:

❖ The Sleuth Kit: This tool is designed to investigate and analyse digital forensics and identify security breaches. It provides forensic analysis of compromised systems.

❖ Volatility: This is an open source memory analysis tool used to assess system attacks through analysis of dumped memory. It can identify running processes, task lists, and memory allocation.

❖ Autopsy: This is a digital forensics platform used to examine and analyse files and systems to identify security risks and breaches. It assists with forensic data analysis and covers a range of forensic disciplines.

Security information and event management (SIEM) tools:

❖ OSSIM: This is an open source security information and event management (SIEM) platform that integrates with many other open source security tools. It provides visualization and correlation of security events and alerts.

❖ ELK Stack: This is an open source tool that enables users to index, search, and visualize large volumes of data. It can be used to extract security event information from multiple sources and collate into a coherent report.

❖ Security Onion: This is an open source intrusion detection system (IDS) that integrates multiple open source security tools. It specializes in detecting data breaches, intrusion, and other security issues.

Best practices for using open source tools

While open source tools can be a useful resource for computer security professionals, there are some best practices that users should follow to maximize their effectiveness and security.

➤ Keep updated: Like many tools in the technology space, open source tools are continually updated to enhance their functionality and address potential vulnerabilities. It's critical that users keep their software versions up-to-date.

➤ Review the code: Open source tools' underlying code is often available to view. To detect any potential security gaps, security professionals should review the code regularly, look for vulnerabilities, and explore potential security risks.

➤ Verify software integrity: Before installing an open source tool or downloading an update, security professionals should verify that the software package has not been modified or damaged during transmission.

➤ Use caution when downloading: There are many websites purporting to offer open source tools. However, not all of them are legitimate, and many fake websites are designed to distribute malware or other harmful programs. Users should only download software from trusted sources that have verified the authenticity of the tool.

➤ Employ hardening practices: Hardening practices involve configuring software to minimize potential vulnerabilities.

Security professionals should implement hardening practices when using open source tools to minimize potential security risks.

Conclusion

Using open source security tools can be an excellent way for computer security professionals to bolster cybersecurity measures without incurring significant expenses. However, it's important to take precautions to ensure the software is authentic, up-to-date, and free from vulnerabilities. By following best practice guidelines and keeping open source tools updated, security professionals can make the most of these resources and reduce potential security risks.

CHAPTER 17: CAREER OPPORTUNITIES IN COMPUTER SECURITY

As technology continues to advance, the need for qualified professionals in the cybersecurity field continues to grow. The increasing amount and complexity of computer security threats in organizations of all types and sizes demands a set of knowledgeable and experienced professionals capable of protecting their employers from cyber-attacks. In chapter 17, we will discuss the current state of the job market in the cybersecurity field, the skills required to succeed in the industry, the importance of continuous learning and professional development, and the role of certifications in career progression.

Career Trends

The demand for cybersecurity professionals is expected to grow significantly in the near future, with some estimates predicting a workforce shortage of more than 3 million workers by 2021. This shortage is due to a number of factors, including the increasing reliance of businesses on technology for their operations, the rising number of cyberthreats, and the greater concern for data privacy. The demand is being driven by government agencies, financial institutions, hospitals, law firms, and a variety of other industries.

Skills Required

The cybersecurity field is expansive, so there is a diverse set of required skills for each area within the industry. However, some skills are essential across the board, including:

➢ Understanding of network and system administration

➢ Knowledge of security fundamentals and principles

➢ Understanding of threat management and information security risk assessment

➢ Knowledge of network protocols and architecture

➢ Familiarity with operating systems, databases and web applications

➢ Communication, problem-solving and critical thinking

➢ Knowledge of compliance regulations and laws

Certifications

Professional certifications complement a degree in computer science or information technology and can help enhance job opportunities and pay. Cybersecurity candidates have numerous certification options to harness their technical knowledge and security-related skills. Some of the well-known cybersecurity certifications are:

❖ Certified Information Systems Security Professional (CISSP)

❖ Certified Ethical Hacker (CEH)

❖ CompTIA Security+

❖ GIAC Information Security Professional (GISP)

❖ Certified Cyber Security Professional (CCSP)

Career Paths

There are different career paths within cybersecurity, so professionals can advance to roles that suit their interests and skills. A few popular career paths include:

➢ Penetration Testing - Responsible for identifying vulnerabilities or gaps in the organization's security posture, a career in Penetration Testing requires knowledge in web applications, cloud technologies, operating systems, and social engineering techniques.

➢ Security Analyst - The role of security analysts is to monitor network activity for potential threats and develop strategies for ensuring the overall safety and security of information systems. Candidates are required to have both technical and problem-solving skills.

➢ Security Consultant - Responsible for advising businesses on how to manage risk and protect their technology infrastructure from potential threats. Security consultants must possess a deep understanding of the barriers to achieve the cybersecurity posture and be able to articulate and execute on resolution options.

➢ Security Architect - Security architects are responsible for creating and implementing security measures across an organization's digital infrastructure. They are required to have knowledge in networking, databases, software, systems and security fundamentals.

Education and Training options

To enter the cybersecurity field a Bachelor of Science in Information Technology, Computer Science or Cybersecurity is a good start. Also, numerous education training and scholarships are being offered by governmental agencies, businesses or cybersecurity organizations. these programs cover the basic fundamentals and provide hands-on experience in the industry.

Professional Development

Professional development is crucial in the cybersecurity industry. The rapid rate of technological advancements and new threats means that professionals must be continually learning to stay ahead of the curve. Joining professional security-related groups, attending industry conferences, participating in webinars, receiving regular updates from industry professionals, and reading industry-related publications are just a few ways to keep abreast of the latest in the industry.

Conclusion

The computer security industry has a high growth rate, making cybersecurity a lucrative career path for IT professionals. Becoming a cybersecurity professional involves honing technical and soft skills, obtaining certifications, and continuously learning about the industry's trends. Whether an IT professional is just starting a career or transitioning to cybersecurity, the industry has a place for everyone.

CHAPTER 18: ETHICAL AND LEGAL ASPECTS OF COMPUTER SECURITY

As computer security becomes more important in our daily lives, there are moral and legal considerations that must be addressed. In this chapter, we will explore the concept of ethical and legal aspects of computer security. We will discuss ethical considerations in security research and practice, responsible disclosure and vulnerability reporting, legal regulations and frameworks for computer security, and balancing security and privacy in emerging technologies.

Ethical Considerations in Security Research and Practice

As the field of computer security grows, so do the questions around the ethics involved in conducting research and practice. One of the primary ethical considerations in this field is the question of whether or not safety and perceived privacy of users and businesses should be sacrificed for the sake of advancing research or developing better security measures.

There is also a question of ethical research methods. Security researchers have an ethical obligation to conduct research in a way that protects the privacy and confidentiality of their subjects.

Researchers must also disclose the risks and potential harms of their research and seek informed consent from their subjects.

Another ethical consideration is the use of exploits or vulnerabilities in applications and systems. Some argue that the use of these flaws in security to develop better security measures or conduct ethical hacking is justified while others argue it is not, as it is still considered illegal under the Computer Fraud and Abuse Act.

Responsible Disclosure and Vulnerability Reporting

Responsible disclosure is the process through which security researchers report vulnerabilities to the vendor or organization responsible for the software or system that the vulnerability affects. The responsible disclosure process allows the vendor or organization to fix the issue before it can be exploited by malicious actors.

There has been much debate about the responsible disclosure process, primarily who should be responsible for it and how long it should take. Some argue that vendors and organizations should be responsible for the process and should be provided with ample time to fix the vulnerability before it is publicly disclosed. Others argue that the vulnerability should be shared with the public as soon as possible to ensure that users are aware of the risks.

Legal Regulations and Frameworks for Computer Security

In addition to ethical considerations, there are also legal regulations and frameworks that address computer security practices. One of the most well-known is the Computer Fraud and Abuse Act (CFAA), which addresses the unauthorized access of a computer system or the theft or damage of data. There are also numerous state, federal, and international regulations that regulate data privacy, like GDPR in Europe, CCPA in California, and HIPAA for medical records in the US.

There are also ethical hacking laws that affect security researchers. These laws protect security researchers from prosecution if they report a vulnerability in a product or system as long as they do not cause excessive harm.

Balancing Security and Privacy in Emerging Technologies

Emerging technologies like artificial intelligence and blockchain have the potential to revolutionize security measures but also have the potential to interfere with our privacy. With the advancement of technologies like facial recognition and IoT, concerns have been raised regarding the collection and use of personal data.

There is a challenge in balancing the need for better security measures and protecting user privacy. As new technologies continue to emerge, policymakers, vendors, and organizations must work together to strike a balance between improving security measures and protecting user privacy.

Conclusion

In conclusion, the ethical and legal considerations in computer security are critical in the development and practice of security measures. Security researchers must consider whether their research and practice are ethical, disclose vulnerabilities responsibly, and comply with laws and regulations relevant to their field. Additionally, policymakers and organizations must balance the need for better security measures and the protection of user privacy, particularly as new technologies continue to emerge. By addressing ethical and legal considerations in computer security, we can improve security measures for everyone.

CHAPTER 19:
CASE STUDIES IN
COMPUTER SECURITY

Real-world examples of security breaches and their impact

Computer security is becoming increasingly important as technology advances and more personal and sensitive data is stored digitally. Unfortunately, cyber-crime is also advancing, targeting individuals, businesses, and governments alike. In this chapter, we will look at some notable cases of security breaches and the effects they had on the victims. We will also examine the root causes and vulnerabilities that led to these incidents, and the lessons we can learn from them.

Target

In December 2013, Target, one of the largest retail chains in the United States, suffered a massive data breach that exposed the personal and financial information of over 110 million customers. The hackers gained access to Target's payment processing system through a vulnerability in its vendor management system. The attackers launched their attack through a phishing email that contained a link to a malware-laced website.

The fallout from the breach was severe. Target's reputation was damaged, its stock price fell, and it faced numerous lawsuits. It was later found that Target had not implemented adequate security protocols, had poor network segmentation, and had outdated software. The company introduced new policies and procedures and invested heavily in upgrading its systems to prevent a repeat of the incident.

Equifax

In 2017, Equifax, one of the largest credit bureaus in the United States, suffered a data breach that exposed the personal information of 143 million individuals. The breach occurred due to a vulnerability in an open-source software called Apache Struts. Despite being alerted to the vulnerability, Equifax failed to patch its systems in time, allowing the attackers to exploit the security hole.

The fallout from the breach was significant. Equifax faced criticism for its slow response, poor security practices, and lack of transparency. The breach led to numerous lawsuits and the resignation of several senior executives. Equifax instituted new security measures and invested in new technology to prevent similar incidents in the future.

Yahoo

In 2013 and 2014, Yahoo suffered two massive data breaches that exposed the personal information of over 3 billion user accounts. The attacks were carried out by state-sponsored hackers and were not discovered until 2016, after Verizon Communications had acquired Yahoo.

The fallout from the breaches was devastating for Yahoo. Its stock price fell, and it received criticism for its poor security practices and lack of transparency. The company was forced to disclose the breaches and faced numerous lawsuits from affected users. In 2019, a settlement was reached where Yahoo agreed to pay $117.5 million to victims of the data breaches.

NotPetya

Not all cyber-attacks are aimed at stealing sensitive data or financial gain. In June 2017, the NotPetya malware was unleashed, affecting organizations globally, but particularly in Ukraine. The malware was disguised as ransomware, but its real goal was destruction. NotPetya targeted communications networks, state infrastructure, and businesses, causing widespread disruption and financial losses.

NotPetya was later attributed to a Russian military intelligence unit, meaning it was a state-sponsored attack. It highlighted the risks of cyber-warfare and the need for countries and organizations to implement robust security measures to counter such threats.

WannaCry

In May 2017, WannaCry ransomware infected over 200,000 computers in more than 150 countries. The malware exploited a vulnerability in Microsoft Windows that had been exploited by the US National Security Agency but had been leaked publicly. The attackers demanded payment in Bitcoin to release the encrypted data.

The WannaCry attack highlighted the importance of patching systems and keeping software up-to-date. It also illustrated the importance of having robust backup systems in place in case of a ransomware attack.

Lessons Learned and Looking Ahead

The cases discussed above demonstrate the devastating consequences of security breaches, both in terms of financial losses and reputational damage. They also highlight the importance of implementing best practices in computer security, such as vulnerability assessments, patch management, and secure coding.

As technology continues to evolve, new security risks will emerge, and organizations will need to stay vigilant to protect themselves and their customers. Collaboration and information sharing among organizations will be crucial to staying ahead of threats, as will investing in new technologies such as artificial intelligence and machine learning.

Ultimately, computer security requires a holistic approach that involves people, processes, and technology. It requires the commitment of organizations to prioritize security, invest in training and education, and implement best practices consistently. If we can do this, we can create a safer digital world for everyone.

CHAPTER 20: CONCLUSION AND FUTURE DIRECTIONS IN COMPUTER SECURITY

As we come to the end of this book, we hope that you have gained a good understanding of computer security, its importance, and the threats that we face. We have explored various types of security threats, vulnerabilities, and exploits, along with their corresponding countermeasures. We have also discussed the key principles of authentication and access control, network security, application security, mobile device security, cloud security, social media security, IoT security, incident response and recovery, risk management and compliance, security culture, open-source tools for security, career opportunities in security, ethical and legal considerations in security, and case studies in security.

Looking ahead, the field of computer security is constantly evolving, and we are likely to see new and more sophisticated threats emerge. For example, as technology continues to advance, we can expect to see more targeted cyber-attacks, including quantum-based cryptography attacks, hardware-based side-channel attacks that exploit microprocessor vulnerabilities like Spectre and Meltdown, and attacks that use machine learning and artificial intelligence to bypass security controls.

To address these evolving threats, it is important that we continue to develop new and innovative security solutions. For example, technologies such as blockchain, homomorphic encryption, and post-quantum cryptography may play an important role in securing our systems and data.

Additionally, as more and more devices become connected through the Internet of Things, we need to pay special attention to securing these devices, which may lack the necessary hardware and software resources to adequately protect themselves. We must also work to develop stronger privacy policies and regulations, especially in light of recent events such as the Cambridge Analytica scandal, which raises serious concerns about personal data privacy.

In conclusion, computer security is a constantly evolving field that requires ongoing vigilance and improvement. As technology continues to advance, it is up to us as individuals, businesses, and society as a whole to stay informed about new security threats and technologies, and to take appropriate measures to protect ourselves and our data. We hope that this book has provided you with a solid foundation in computer security, and that it has inspired you to continue learning and exploring this critical field. Remember, by working together, we can make our digital world a safer and more secure place.

Final Thoughts

I hope this Computer Security Guide has been informative and helpful in providing you with the knowledge and tools necessary to protect your digital life. Remember, the internet can be a dangerous place filled with potential threats aimed at compromising your personal information and sensitive data.

By implementing the tips and strategies outlined in this book, you can confidently navigate the online world while reducing your risk of falling victim to cybercrime. Simple steps such as regularly updating software, enabling two-factor authentication, using strong passwords, and avoiding suspicious emails or websites can go a long way in safeguarding your devices and networks.

It is also important to maintain a healthy level of scepticism when it comes to online interactions. Always verify the authenticity of requests for personal information or financial transactions before providing any details. Trust your instincts and take steps to protect yourself from phishing scams and other malicious attacks.

Finally, stay informed about emerging threats and evolving security measures by following reputable sources online. With continued vigilance and awareness, you can stay one step ahead of cybercriminals and enjoy all that the digital world has to offer with peace of mind.

ABOUT THE AUTHOR

Ray Goodwin

Ray Goodwin, is the author behind this series of captivating books on Business Development and self improvement, and has left an indelible mark on the field. He was born and raised in the bustling city of London, where he developed a strong work ethic and an insatiable curiosity about the inner workings of successful businesses. Throughout his illustrious career, Ray leveraged his extensive knowledge and experience to help numerous companies flourish and prosper.

His keen insights and innovative strategies has earned him recognition, driving him to share his expertise with others. Ray believes in the power of sharing knowledge to elevate businesses and empower aspiring entrepreneurs.

Ray's dedication to his craft is evident in the numerous books he has authored on business development and self improvement. His writing style seamlessly blends practical advice, thought-provoking concepts, and real-life case studies, making his books invaluable resources for business professionals and novices alike. His ability to distill complex concepts into accessible language has greatly impacted the lives and careers of countless individuals.

Now retired from the corporate world, Ray and his beloved wife have settled in the idyllic English countryside. Surrounded by the beauty of nature, Ray finds inspiration for his writing and indulges in his hobbies.

Ray Goodwin's books continue to serve as enduring guides for those seeking success in the business world. With a wealth of experience and a deep understanding of the inner workings of businesses, Ray's work remains a testament to his passion for sharing knowledge and helping others flourish.

www.ingramcontent.com/pod-product-compliance
Lightning Source LLC
LaVergne TN
LVHW051714050326
832903LV00032B/4201